THE APARTHEID REGIME IN THE STATE OF ISRAEL -

THE BIG LIE IS EXPOSED

Credit for the cover photo: © Nsilcock | Dreamstime Stock

Tel: +97254-8030648

Email: kobimnsil@gmail.com

Web site: www.kobisha.com

CLARIFICATION

On 14/11/2015 a far reaching decision was made to label products that have been manufactured in the settlements and in the Golan Heights by a special tag. In terms of the European Union this is a deserving punishment to an occupying country that applies apartheid against the Palestinians.

Two days later, on 17/11/2015, a brutal terror attack was committed in the City of Lights – Paris, located in the heart of Europe. Ostensibly these two events are not connected but in fact they are one. The inability to connect between the events, the use of double standards regarding anything related to Israel and to the rest of the world is what eventually leads also to the outbreak of a wave of internal terrorism. Labeling the products is therefore a reward for terrorism the guiding ideology of which is based on sheer anti-Semitism, on double standards and on unlimited hatred. This is not the first time that Europe labels the Jews and the self-righteous ones will say that this is not the case and that the reasons are justified. But in fact, and I shall prove it to you in this book how the industry of hate and anti-Semitism seeks any possible way to try and destroy the Jewish state. After all, if the problem is a problem of borders and of occupied territory and therefore punitive measures are taken against the cruel conqueror then please Europe put us on hold until you finish to solve the problem of the borders in Cyprus and the dispute concerning Gibraltar that has been going on for over 200 years. The demarcation of the borders between the State of Israel and the Palestinians will, in the end, be determined by negotiation. I am sure most of you have not heard that there have already been a number of attempts to give up all the territory in favor of the Palestinians but wonder of wonders the Palestinians refused!

It seems that I have chosen harsh words to describe this situation but does anyone of the readers actually know what a settlement is? Is anyone of the readers knowledgeable about the intricacies of the conflict? Does anyone of the readers know who the real conqueror is and who is the vanquished? Is anyone of the readers aware of the fact that mostly Palestinians are employed in these factories in the "settlements" and that this resolution will lead to a situation where many factories will close and then reopen within the Green Line leaving dozens of Palestinians out of work! Did you know that? Did you know that the settlements are in the West Bank historically known as "Judea and Samaria"? Is the name Judea an Arab name or a Jewish one?

In this book I shall reveal to you the hypocrisy that is inherent in the whole issue of apartheid and the witch-hunt that is going on around the State of Israel, out of the intent to harm it in any possible way even at the expense of the Palestinians. After all, the core of the conflict is not about "occupied territories" since the area of the State of Israel is 0.15% of the area of the Middle East; this is a religious war, the same religious war that is taking place on the poor and innocent European soil, that is doing everything in its power to weaken the State of Israel by boycotts, denunciations, and donations to Muslim "charities" that use this money to acquire weapons and enthusiastic soldiers.

And if, however, I did not manage to convince you about the lie machine and the propaganda that are raging against the tiny Jewish state, the only democracy in the Middle East, the ancient homeland of the Jewish people for over 3,000 years, 1,600 before Mohammad came to the world, then you are welcome to boycott Israel, and in order to do this in an optimal way I attach a guide that will teach you how to boycott the State of Israel. Read it to the end and then boycott as much as you want please!

About the author

Kobi Shashoua is an author and a lecturer. Among his books you can find the most comprehensive book that exists to date bout the Israeli-Palestinian conflict "Israel: the truth, the whole truth and nothing but the truth." This book leads the reader chapter by chapter through the complex reality of the conflict and dissects the causes for the crisis, uncovers to the reader the true faces of the parties involved, and presents the tactics, the strategies and the true objectives, that lie below the surface. The author also wrote the book series: "Understanding the Middle East".The book you are holding in your hands is from that series.

The author, who resides in Israel, which is located in the most dangerous neighborhood of the world, in the heart of the Middle East, shares with us the facts together with the insights and the unique understanding of the region where he lives. We invite you to take part in this journey from a safe distance.

TABLE OF CONTENTS

THE RACIAL APARTHEID POLICY OF THE ZIONIST REGIME

The Israeli apartheid is so bad and despicable that the need arose to commemorate it annually during a whole week. This event is worldwide and it occurs in many countries around the globe where it is celebrated in all its glory in many universities and in major cities around the world. I counted 88 such cities out of the official website http://apartheidweek.org. Had it only been the annual number of countries that commemorate the Week of Global Warming......

The objectives of each event in the website are specified:

Israeli Apartheid Week (IAW) is an international series of events that seeks to raise awareness about Israel's apartheid policies towards the Palestinians and to build support for the growing Boycott, Divestment, and Sanctions (BDS) campaign.

Map of participating cities

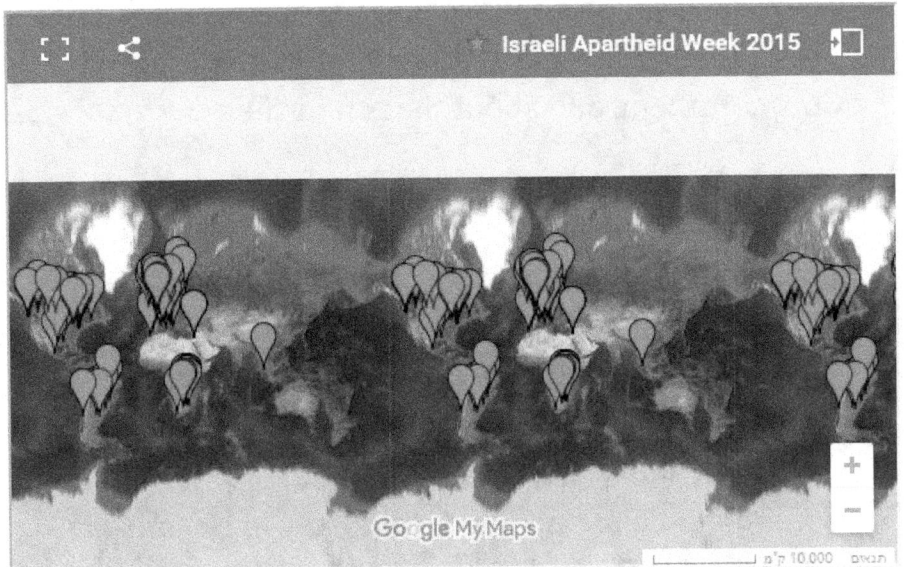

From the website – list of the cities that commemorate the Israeli Apartheid Week. It is heartwarming to realize that there is global solidarity on this subject. Now help me harness this solidarity to human rights and women rights in the Muslim world.

I suppose it works for them in Europe since in the first stage products from "the occupied territories" have been labeled as such. I would like to join in this book the objectives of the website and arouse the awareness on the subject of "apartheid" in the State of Israel and to provide also information about companies that are connected to the State of Israel so that you could boycott them, and about that on further reading…………

Well, as I mentioned, this week denotes the policy of apartheid that the State of Israel conducts against the Palestinians, and its purpose is to arouse the awareness to the subject among the citizens of the world. The organizers hope that just as an international awakening and international pressure led eventually to the end of apartheid in South Africa, the "apartheid" that prevails in the State of Israel will come to an end [1]. In principle, they are right. But there is a small problem: **there is no apartheid in Israel!**

MAKES NO SENSE!

Apparently I am lying. Otherwise what? So much is invested in denouncing the apartheid regime in Israel just for nothing?

But let me ask an honest question: what the hell is apartheid? Sometimes I watch programs on TV where regular citizens all over the globe are asked about essential matters. The most customary answers of most people amount to answers such as "It's pretty cool man", "That's nice". The level of superficiality and of understanding of acute issues does not compare to the control many people have in Facebook, YouTube, and in using the IPhone. Had the situation been reversed, there would have been no need for this book in order to expose the lies and the tricks of the global propaganda machinery that conducts a campaign against the Jewish people by attacking the State of Israel 24/7.

Let's check where does the term apartheid derive from:

According to Wikipedia, "Apartheid (in Africans: Apartheid – segregation) is the policy and the racist regime applied by the white minority Government in South Africa from 1948 until 1990. This policy was based on racial segregation between whites, blacks and colored (mixed descent), and on granting privileges to the white minority. Since the early 60`s, the policy of apartheid has been increasingly condemned by the international community, a process that led gradually to the excommunication of South Africa from the family of nations, and to the imposition of sanction against it. These, combined with severe internal unrest on the part of the resistance to apartheid organizations, led eventually to the collapse, after four decades, of the apartheid regime in a peaceful process and through an orderly transfer of power to the black majority in democratic elections".

---

(1) I shall tell you in secrecy and diverge from the purpose of this book that their final goal is not only to bring the "apartheid" in Israel to an end but to bring Israel to an end......

In practical terms, blacks were forbidden to vote or to be elected in the general elections. They were forbidden to study in the universities and to get medical treatment in hospitals for white people. Blacks were expelled from cities of white people, marriage or intimate relationships between blacks and whites were prohibited, blacks were forbidden to use buses for white people.

For comparison, I built a tabulation that shows the great similarity between the policy of apartheid in South Africa in the years 1948-1990 and the current "apartheid" policy in the State of Israel:

The apartheid regime in South Africa	The apartheid regime in Israel
It is forbidden to vote in the general elections	Arab citizens vote for the Israeli Knesset
It is forbidden to be elected in the general elections	In the 20th Knesset that was elected on 17/03/15 there are 15 Arab Knesset members
Blacks are forbidden to study in universities	Arab citizen study in all the universities in the State of Israel
Blacks are forbidden to get medical treatment in hospitals for white people	Arab citizen get medical treatment in all the hospitals in the State of Israel
Blacks are forbidden to use busses for white people	Arab citizens are allowed full freedom of action like any citizen in the State of Israel
Blacks are discriminated in all levels of life	Arab citizens have full equality of rights
	An Arab judge is serving in the Supreme Court
	In 1999 an Arab woman was elected Miss Israel

Conclusion: they are fooling us again! In the State of Israel there has never been and there will never be an apartheid regime. The State of Israel is the only country in the Middle East where Arab citizens can be elected to parliament and to the government democratically in the general elections.[2]!

Arab citizens are full-fledged members of the Knesset and even take advantage of their electoral power to harm the State of Israel where they live.   The most prominent example is that of the former Knesset Member Azmi Bishara. In 2001 Bishara attended the memorial of Hafez al-Assad [3] in Syria, where the Secretary General of the Hezbollah [4] was also present.

Bishara called upon the Palestinians to continue their struggle against the State of Israel. As a result, the Israeli Central Elections Committee for the 16th Knesset disqualified him from running again, but the Supreme Court of Israel re-qualified him to run for office again. What is this if not democracy!

His misdeeds included also encouraging violence in the events of October 2000 [5], but since he was an elected official, he enjoyed immunity.

MAKES NO SENSE!

---

[2] Except Syria, of course.

[3] President of Syria in 1970-2000.

[4] More can be found under the entry "Azmi Bishara" in Wikipedia.

[5] "The October 2000 events were a wave of violent riots and demonstrations of Israeli Arabs that broke out in early October 2000 in close proximity to the break out of the second Intifada. During the events 13 Israeli Arabs demonstrators were killed and one Palestinian that was not an Israeli citizen, as well as one Israeli Jew who got killed from throwing stones". From Wikipedia, under "The events of October 2000".

When he was member of the Knesset he used to go on visits to Syria and to Lebanon, despite the prohibition to visit an enemy country. Therefore, his immunity was removed in 2001 and he was indicted. In September 2006 he visited Damascus. During his visit he met with the Syrian President Bashar al-Assad, and stated that he supports Syrian`s struggle against the State of Israel. The Attorney General of Israel considered opening a criminal investigation against him.

On April 8th 2007 it was published that Bashara left Israel without specifying the circumstances. On April 22 Bashara submitted a letter of resignation from the Knesset to the Israeli consul in Cairo.

Following the removal of the gagging order on May 2nd 2007, it became known that an investigation against Bashara has been conducted on suspicions that during the Second Lebanon war he contacted a Hezbollah agent and provided him with information that undermined the security of the State of Israel: the adjustment of missiles fire, the effect of increasing the range of the missiles beyond Haifa, assessments regarding the assassination attempts of the Hezbollah Secretary General etc.

According to allegations, he received hundreds of thousands of shekels from Hezbollah and from other foreign bodies for supplying the information, while transgressing the Anti Money Laundering and Terror Funding Prohibition Law.

The conclusion is clear. Not only unlike an apartheid regime, where blacks were not allowed to be elected in the general elections, in the State of Israel the Arabs have full equal rights that allow them to be elected to the Knesset and act from there under the Immunity Law and ex officio, even to harm the State of Israel from within – this is not apartheid, this is a Trojan horse!

A Trojan Horse Was Found!

There is no reason to panic, though. Try to follow the given advice and links.

Does it make sense to anyone that a representative of the American Congress or the Senate will go and meet representatives of the Taliban/Al-Qaeda/ISIS and encourage them to continue to fight the Unites States?

Is there any apartheid here?

Is this what apartheid means?

Apartheid indeed exists in Israel, but it is directed against the Jewish and the Christian religions and even with the knowledge of the Israeli government:

The Western Wall is the only one that survived the destruction of the Second Temple. The Western Wall is the holiest place to the Jews. On the ruins of the Temple the "Al- Aqsa" mosque was constructed, founded in 679 AD. "Temple Mount" [6] is located in an area controlled by the State of Israel and still there are restrictions to worshipers.

During the summer, non-Muslims are allowed to enter the site between 8:30-11:30 and 13:30-14:30. During winter everything moves one hour back. Admission to Jews is possible through one gate only – the Mugreb gate. Muslims are allowed to enter whenever they wish, through several gates. It is forbidden to bring to Temple Mount a prayer book (Siddur), a Bible, a festival prayer book Mchzor), a prayer shawl, and a ram's horn (shofar). In addition, it is forbidden to participate in any religious activity. **This ban does not apply to Muslims**.

This is the only religious apartheid that is imposed in Israel and it is against the Jews.

MAKES NO SENSE!

(6) Temple Mount is located on Mount Moriah in Jerusalem. Here King Solomon built the First Temple in the middle of the 10th century BC. In 586 BC it was destroyed by Nebuchadnezzar, King of Babylon. 70 years after the First Destruction the second Temple was built by the pilgrims from Babylon with the assistance of King Herod. The Second Temple was destroyed in 70 AD by Titus the Roman Emperor. Since then no new Temple was built. Temple Mount is the holiest place for Jews. On its ruins two Muslim structures were built since the 7th AD – the Al Aqsa Mosque and the Dome of the Rock.

And now to a different place: some might say that in fact I mislead the reader, and the question that may arise by itself will be whether Israel is imposing a policy of apartheid against the Palestinians held in the occupied territories?

Well, the West Bank and the Gaza Strip have never been annexed to the State of Israel. This is a territory defined as the "occupied territories". The Palestinians who live there have never been, and are not today either, Israeli citizens. Therefore, the use of the term apartheid is not only out of place, but a rude and cynical attempt to distort reality and to convince those who are unaware of the facts that this is apartheid.

"The occupied territories" were not captured from the Palestinians. They were captured during the Six Days War, when the Arab countries tried to accomplish the liquidation of the State of Israel and throw the Jews into the sea.

As mentioned, not only did the plan fail, but the State of Israel triumphed over the Arab countries that fought against it and conquered from Egypt the entire Sinai Peninsula, which it willingly returned as part of the peace agreement with Egypt signed in 1979, the Golan Heights from Syria, and the West Bank from Jordan.

How did the areas conquered from these countries become, over the years, Palestinian territories? And why did the Palestinians not say a word over the years, when these territories were a sovereign part of Egypt and of Jordan?

This illustration shows the State of Israel after the War of Independence in 1948. The occupied territories - Judea and Samaria that are called today the West Bank – were an integral part of Jordan, and the Gaza Strip was an integral part of Egypt.

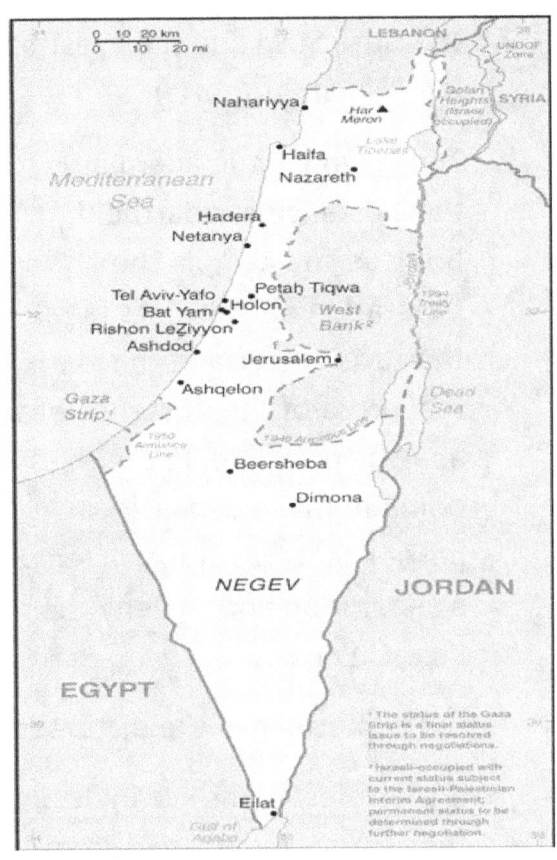

In 1988 Jordan announced the detachment of this region from the country. In the peace agreement with Egypt the Egyptians, as well, refused to get back the Gaza Strip, their territory. These territories were left, in fact, without sovereignty and the geographic facts dictated the need to establish a Palestinian state in the "occupied territories". The Hamas terror organization rules the Gaza Strip and the West bank is ruled by the Palestinian Authority.

Those who argue adamantly for the existence of apartheid, bring as an example the separation barrier.[7] As far as they are concerned, this is a real proof of the existence of an apartheid regime. In their opinion, this is a malicious  barrier that was constructed with the aim to make a separation and to deny the rights of the Palestinians.

But something in the picture is not clear.

If the Palestinians live in occupied territories and the State of Israel builds a security barrier, is this a separation barrier that separates citizens of the same country, or maybe it is a barrier designed to separate the areas of the State of Israel from the Palestinians territories? Building a barrier is part of the responsibility of the State of Israel to protect its citizens from massacres of innocent people.

The State of Israel recognized the solution of two states for two peoples and the removal of barriers is conditional on the cessation of terrorism. The military operations of Israel in the territories of the West Bank are defensive operations intended to prevent the terror organizations from committing attacks in Israel. Were it not for the terror attacks, there would be no need for military operations in the West Bank.

Remember again the saying: On the day the Arabs lay down their weapon there will be peace, but on the day Israel lays down its weapon, it will cease to exist!

The West Bank is not part of Israel, and Israel has declared that it has no intention to annex the whole area. The purpose of the barrier is to separate and to prevent the Palestinian terror from penetrating into Israel and from killing innocent civilians.

(7) One of the many cartoons that show the separation barrier in a negative way. The message here is clear: once again the State of Israel blatantly tramples rights.

By the way, the United States has set up a barrier between its borders and Mexico in order to prevent the infiltration of illegal immigrants.

In 2004 the International Court of Justice in Hague ruled that the construction of the barrier, [8] set up to prevent the infiltration of suicide bombers into Israel, is contrary to International law. The Court called upon Israel to stop building the barrier in the Palestinian occupied territories, including East Jerusalem and its surroundings. Whatever has been built should be destroyed and of course to pay compensation as well. The Court also called upon the international community to take legal means in order to stop further construction and the violations committed by the State of Israel.

[8] From Wikipedia under "The separation barrier".

In short, it seems that as far as Israel is concerned, all its actions are contrary to International law.

The Israeli government rejected the ruling and announced that it would continue   to build the barrier. The International Court of Justice chose to ignore the terror attacks committed against Israelis. Factually, the barrier prevented many terror attacks.

As usual, in the field of hypocrisy there are no fences. The jury was composed of Chinese judges (China occupied Tibet), of Russians (who conducted a brutal all-out war in Chechnya and have lately occupied the Crimea peninsula) and of Jordanian judges (Jordan slaughtered Palestinians in the operation "Black September"). These are the judges who judge Israel!

MAKES NO SENSE!

The barrier has prevented, among other things, the recurrence of events like those shown in these photos:

Search and rescue teams evacuate parts of bodies from the remains of a bus on line 18 blown up by a suicide bomber in Jerusalem, 25.02.96.

Photo: Heidi Milner, The Government Press Office.

Parts of bodies in the remains of a sooty bus
blown up by a suicide bomber on line 18 in
Jerusalem, 03.03.96. Please note that this is the
second attack on the same line within a few days.

Photo: Avi Ohayon, The Government Press Office.

A police officer and a civilian bend over a person wounded in a suicide bombing attack on a busy street in central Jerusalem, March 21st, 2002. Photo: Flash 90.

All of that would not have happened, of course, had it not been for the fulfillment of the aspiration of the parents and of the leaders of the "Palestinian" people to educate and train their children to achieve their mission as Shahids.

 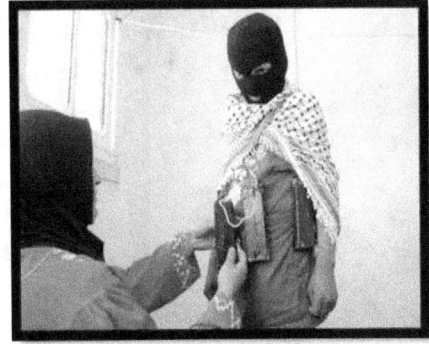

(AP Photo/Israeli Army/HO) (10)   (9)

(9) This photo was displayed in the Facebook page of Fatah, alongside an imaginary dialogue between the child who was sent to his death, and the mother who encourages this. "Why me and not you?" the child asks his mother, and she answers him that she will continue to bear children "for Palestine". Translation by the research institute "Palestinian Media Watch." http://www.palwatch.org.il

(10) The picture of the baby dressed as a suicide bomber is a photo of a Palestine baby wearing a devise similar to an explosive belt found during a search by the IDF soldiers in a house in Hebron on the 29th of June 2002. See further details on that under "Photo of the baby dressed up as a suicide bomber", in Wikipedia.

The International Court of Justice in Hague did not seem to be baffled in light of these facts.

Is the barrier indeed fulfilling its main function – to prevent the infiltration of   terrorist cells into the State of Israel?

The following slide indicates that the barrier has prevented significantly the ability of terror organizations to infiltrate into the country.

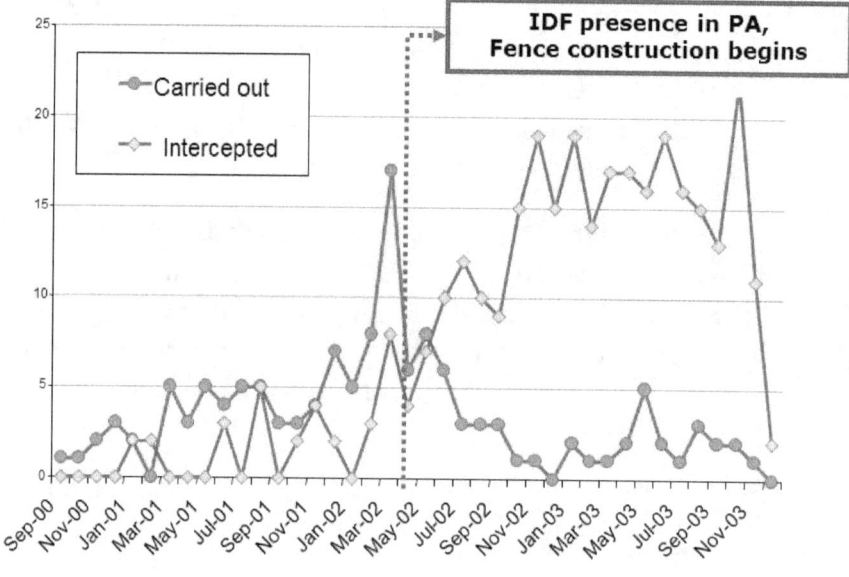

The slide is from a presentation kept at the Israeli Foreign Ministry. [11]

Until the construction of the barrier, the amount of terror attacks in the State of Israel was on a daily basis. Wherever there was a public gathering was a legitimate target, especially if there were women and children. The construction of the barrier has helped to reduce drastically the number of Israelis killed as a result of terror attacks. The following graph illustrates this better than the written words:

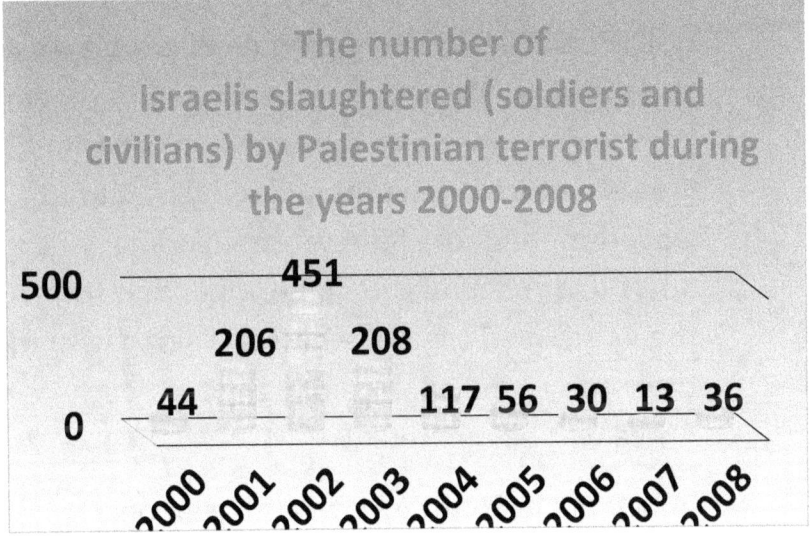

The data was taken from the website: www.theisraelproject.org

---

(11) Securityfence.mfa.gov.il/mfm/Data/49058

We must always bear in mind that the outline of the separation barrier is designed to act as a buffer between the State of Israel and the Palestinian Authority. The barrier is not in the territory of the State of Israel and does not separate different populations within it. Setting up a separating barrier between different entities is customary in many regions in the world. We shall refer to it further on. This is not apartheid! The whole purpose is to utilize once again the ignorance of people, the superficiality, the lack of interest and to repeat the message over and over again in order to create de facto – an unfounded fact that the Government in the State of Israel is an apartheid rule and should be wiped out from the world (and the State of Israel along with it), the same as the apartheid regime in South Africa was eliminated.

Apartheid in South Africa was based on separation of races and colors, between the ruling white man and the subjected black person. In the State of Israel there is a full equality of rights between Jews and Arabs and the general population. The irony is that in no Arab country out of the vast number of Arab countries the Arabs have equal rights, except for Syria of course!!!

The State of Israel has set up a security barrier around the Gaza Strip as well. Israel evacuated from the Gaza Strip its last soldiers and civilians. The result is a nest of terrorism controlled by Hamas and a trickling of other terror organizations such as al-Qaeda. The aim of Hamas is to wipe out the State of Israel, and it is affiliated much more with Iran and the Hezbollah than its Palestinian brothers in the occupied territories in the West Bank, which is Judea and Samaria.

Remember, the whole purpose is to undermine the legitimacy of the Jewish people in their historic homeland, where they have been living thousands of years before the advent of what is called – Islam.

In the Middle East apartheid exists among the Arab countries.

The separation of roads is sometimes discussed in connection with the term apartheid, when the issue is the roads where only Jews are allowed to drive. But what do you say about roads in Saudi Arabia where religious apartheid exists: look at the following photos:

An example for the existence of freedom of religious worship for all nations

This is – apartheid.

But who cares, it is in Saudi Arabia and Israel is not connected to it!

And we will conclude as usual with some fascinating facts:

The separation barrier of the atrocious Zionist regime has cut apart the "Palestinian people" and does not allow them to exercise their historical rights. These rights include the will to throw the Jews into the sea and to establish instead a democratic regime, a western, dictatorial, Islamic and extreme, similar to the regime that exists in the Gaza Strip. Therefore, no wonder that the barrier was denounced at the United Nations and was even condemned by the International Court of Justice in Hague.

Israel did not invent the method of building a security barrier – a separation barrier, but it is the only one that was condemned by the Court in Hague. Israel is the only country to where protesters from human rights organizations stream and join their Palestinian counterparts in protest activities. [12]

Hereinafter I will detail a list of barriers that have been built around the world, some by Arab countries that condemn the violation of human rights that Israel has committed by the separation barrier.

Spain and the European Union have set up a barrier between the Spanish enclaves of Ceuta and Melilla on Morocco's sovereign territory in order to prevent the illegal immigration from Morocco and the Sahara (it did not really help them...)

Something to think about: the European Union that condemns the separation barrier built by Israel, has financed a separation barrier within the territory of Morocco (located in Africa) in order to separate between Spanish enclaves and Morocco. Is that not the precise definition for occupied territory?

India has built one of the longest separation barriers in the world. The barrier is about 3,300 kilometers long. The purpose of the barrier is to prevent the entry of Islamic elements from Pakistan into its territory, and to prevent the entry of illegal immigrants from its surrounding countries, such as Bangladesh, Nepal and Burma.

In Cyprus Turkey has built a separation barrier that divides the island into a Turkish controlled area and a Greek controlled area.

Botswana has built a 480 kilometers long barrier as a buffer between it and Zimbabwe, to prevent the entry of refugees escaping from Zimbabwe.

South Korea has constructed a fortified separation barrier between it and its northern neighbor.

Thailand has built a 75 kilometers long barrier between it and Malaysia, to   prevent armed Muslims from crossing into its territory.

Uzbekistan has built a barrier as a buffer between it and Tajikistan.

---

(12) Further details can be found under "Separation barrier" in Wikipedia.

Let us turn now to examples from Arab and Islamic countries that denounce   the "apartheid barrier"!

Saudi Arabia has built a 400 kilometers long barrier on its border with Yemen. In addition, it has built a 900 kilometers long barrier as a buffer between it and neighboring Iraq.

The United Arab Emirates has built separation barrier between it and Oman, Kuwait and Iraq.

Morocco has built a 2,700 kilometers long barrier that separates it from Western Sahara in order to prevent guerilla fighters from penetrating into its territory.

Pakistan has built a 2,400 kilometers long barrier as a buffer between it and Afghanistan and to prevent the infiltration of the Taliban and al-Qaeda into its territory.

Iran has built along its border with Pakistan a 700 kilometers long barrier.

The International Court of Justice in Hague did not find it necessary to intervene in the matter of building these barriers. In fact, most of you did not know that they existed, but the Israeli "Apartheid Barrier" sets a blatant example of abusing human rights!

Israel has announced that if there will be peace between Israel and the Palestinians, it will change the outline of the barrier accordingly.

Think about it, is it not a bit (or a lot) hypocritical to be condemned by countries that have built separation barriers themselves, such as the Arab countries or the European Union?

I emphasize again: the UN General Assembly, where the Arab and the Islamic countries can obtain a majority to any proposal they submit, passed a resolution on December 8th 2003, to apply to the International Court of Justice in Hague for an opinion regarding the barrier that Israel started to build.

The opinion reached, of course, an anti-Israel conclusion. The United States and 22 other western countries maintained that it was a political and not a legal issue.

The Court ruled that the barrier was contrary to international law and that the State of Israel should dismantle it. For some reason, the International Court of Justice chose to ignore the real reason for building this barrier: the atrocious terror attacks launched from the territories of the Palestinian Authority. Setting up the barrier has minimized the number of attacks – up to 98% less.

Next time you hear about the "Israeli Apartheid Week", remember that it is a fiction, just one more trick used in the war between the forces of darkness and the forces of light.

Remember: all that needs to be done for the evil to win is for good people to do nothing.

Despite everything, the barrier was built and serves as a buffer between the Palestinian population and the citizens of the State of Israel. It is an unthinkable act.

So what is left if not to boycott?

About that in the upcoming chapter.

Boycott Israel

Having reviewed and observed with our own eyes how the Zionist entity is   conducting an "apartheid" policy, it is natural to take action and boycott it, exactly as was done to a very similar regime in South Africa.

In fact, boycott of Israel has existed since its establishment and it continues till this very day. In 1945 the Arab countries imposed an economic boycott on the Jewish community and then on the State of Israel that was established in 1948. In 1951, following the resolution of the Arab League that no Arab country should establish economic relations with companies that have commercial relations with the State of Israel, a bureau for the surveillance over the boycott was set up in Damascus. At its peak, about 8,500 companies were banned (including Ford and Coca-Cola), but today the impact of the ban is very low.

The boycott has three aspects: [13]

Boycott of Israeli companies – does not allow export of Israeli products to Arab countries.

Despite the boycott, Israeli products reach Arab countries by exporting to a third country, where all the tags that identify the product as made in Israel are removed and replaced with fictitious tags, that identify the product as the product of the intermediate country. It is difficult to estimate the size of this trade.

Boycott of companies that have business relations with Israel – an aspect that led   many foreign companies (mainly Japanese) to refrain from maintaining any trade relations with Israel. Until the early nineties no Japanese cars were sold in Israel, except for Subaru and Daihatsu that have not surrendered to the boycott.

Boycott of companies that have business relations with Israel – never worked out, probably because of the difficulty to implement it.

Furthermore, there are academic boycotts of universities in the State of Israel by universities in Europe. The leading one is Britain. Researchers and academics who

---

(13) Out of Wikipedia under "The Arab boycott".

are subject to high moral and ethical codes in the field of their research, who examine evidences and draw conclusions in a manner that seeks the truth, in a scientific manner, an unequivocal manner, when it comes to Israel, all the codes of ethics, of scientific research and the pursuit of the truth are void.

Concepts such as apartheid, war crimes, colonialism, racism, occupation are thrown into the air casually. Those academics degrade their institutions and their field of research when they are hypocritical and mean with regard to the State of Israel.

The Arab/Muslim world attacks on all fronts and attempts to destroy the State of Israel: through war, terror, denial of the Holocaust, rewriting history, damage to the economy and through boycotts.

Before I go any further with matters of the boycott, a brief flash on the contribution of Jews to the world:

The number of Jews living today (2015) in the world is 14 million. The world`s population is currently estimated at about 7.3 billion. The number of Muslims is about 1.6 billion. The Jewish population is 0.2% of the world's population.

Nevertheless, the Jews have received over the years Nobel prizes in a significant percentage of their weight in world population. Since the number of Jews who have won the Nobel Prize is very large, I decided to summarize it for you.

As of the end of 2015, the number of the laureates is 194 according to the following distribution: 36 in chemistry, 55 in medicine, 29 in economics, 51 in physics, 14 in literature and another 9 as World Peace winners. [14]

As of 2015, the total number of Nobel Prizes awarded since 1901 is 870. [15]

22% out of all Nobel Prize winners are Jewish, 137 times relative to their ratio of the total population.

---

[14]

http://www.jewishvirtuallibrary.org/jsource/Judaism/nobels.html

(15)

http://www.jewishvirtuallibrary.org/jsource/Judaism/nobels.html

I see it fit to list the names of all the Nobel Prize laureates among the Muslims:[16]

Physics:

1979 - Abdus Salam - Punjabi Ahmadiyya sect

Literature:

1988 - Naguib Mahfouz - Egyptian Muslim

2006 - Orhan Pamuk

Chemistry:

1999 - Ahmed Zewail

2015 - Aziz Sancar

Peace:

1978 - Mohamed Anwar El-Sadat

1994 - Yaser Arafat

2003 - Shirin Ebadi

2005 - Mohamed ElBaradei

2011 - Tawakel Karman

2014 - Malala Yousafzai

The number of awards among the Muslims is 12, with 7 of them of a political nature, that contribute to world peace. A prominent example is the Nobel Prize laureate of 1994, Yasser Arafat, who was awarded the Nobel Peace Prize and continued to wander around wearing his personal gun.

This Nobel Peace Prize winner wrecked the historic peace treaty that could have been concluded with the Palestinians in "Camp David" in 2000 together with Bill Clinton and Ehud Barak. Soon afterwards an incredible wave of terror attacks swept the State of Israel, when suicide bombers started to cast terror daily in the heart of the country.

[16] http://www.jewishmag.com/99mag/nobel/nobel.htm

The irony is that the main component in the total Nobel Prize awards by Muslims is bringing peace to the world – I do not belittle the winners, God forbid, but in fact reality today proves otherwise!

MAKES NO SENSE!

How is a Nobel Prize laureate welcomed in a Muslim country? With honor and glory?

Shirin Ebadi (born in 1947) was awarded the Nobel Peace Prize in 2003, for promoting democracy and human rights in Iran. She was the first Muslim woman to win the prestigious prize. Between the years 1975-1979 she served as the municipal judge in the city of Tehran. In 1979, with the rise of the Ayatollahs to power, she was lowered to a minor post following the decree that a woman cannot serve as a judge. As a pioneer, she has expressed her opinion more than once which included criticism of the Ayatollahs regime, and the same as any "democratic" government would respond – she was sent to jail several times – even after winning the prize!

As a Nobel Prize winner she received benefits from the Ayatollahs government   that included, among other things, blocking her bank account. Funds in her account were transferred in order to assist political prisoners and their families. The medal and the certificate, that were kept safely in the bank vault, were confiscated as well and it seems that the government is making efforts to confiscate her home as well.[17]

In conclusion, it can be said that the Nobel Peace Prize laureate won in Iran the   honor reserved for kings, including appreciation, respect and glory.

MAKES NO SENSE!

---

(17) Further details about the subject can be found on the Ynet website in the article "The Nobel Prize winner from Iran: there is no medal and the bank account was confiscated." (27.11.09)

Winning a Nobel Prize does not occur in a vacuum. The award represents a culminating point in the scientific research or in the performance of the team or of the research/scientific/academic institute. Just imagine that the award is only the tip of the iceberg of human contribution, where thousands of scientists/researchers/academics are members.

This is similar to a marathon race in which tens of thousands participate, but only one reaches the finish line, and yet, each one of the participants is an athlete at heart, with self-discipline and a huge commitment to the cause. Winning a Nobel Prize cannot be achieved without the support and the investment of the research and academic institutions, and without encouraging the cultivation of excellence.

The greatness of the Jewish winners is that they belong to persecuted people that were nearly destroyed, and despite the circumstances, they have managed to overcome the obstacles and achieve the impossible.

The impossible sprouted also in the State of Israel, that over 60 years ago was a desolate desert. Despite being surrounded by many enemies who were doing everything to destroy it, the State has managed to create a "normal atmosphere" among its citizens, and provide a western standard of living in an open, democratic, moral society that is a single and isolated country in a sea of Islamic, dictatorial and totalitarian countries.

The percentage of Muslims out of the world`s population is about 22%. The percentage of the Nobel Prize winners is about 1.37%.

The percentage of Jews out of the world`s population is about 0.2%. The percentage of the Nobel Prize winners is about 1.37 of the total winnings.

If we take the total number of Muslims in the world, and divide it by the total Nobel Prizes they have been awarded, we get: 133,333,333.

If we take the total number of Jews in the world, and divide it by the total Nobel Prizes they have been awarded we get: 72,164.

If we take the two ratios and divide, we get the following number: 1,847. What does that mean? I leave it to your judgment.

A Nobel Prize is guaranteed to whoever solves this correctly!

What is actually the conclusion?

IT SEEMS THAT JEWS CONTROL THE NOBLE PRIZE AWARDS COMMITTEE

As many people think, Israel's main export includes camels, chickens, oranges, carobs and high-rise tents. Unfortunately, large oil deposits, such as our neighbors to the east posses, have not been found yet.

The truth is, it is quite easy to boycott the above products. But I advise those of you who have decided to boycott Israeli export for ideological reasons, to do so out of genuine consciousness and to waive ignorance and superficiality. Therefore, I would like to give you a partial list of products, achievements and contributions to humanity that have been developed in the State of Israel, in order to make it easier for you to boycott.

I collected the data mainly from a Government Information website [19] that is designed to provide tools and insights to anyone who wishes to be an Ambassador of the State of Israel. The website contains enlightening facts that can provide an answer for all the wild and unrestrained incitement that is going on against the State of Israel and the Jews.

Following are excerpts from the website presented in their entirety:

Contribution to world agriculture:

In 1955, Engineer Simcha Blass developed the drip irrigation system.

The drip irrigation system helped to reduce world hunger by increasing crop yields and by saving water.

Further evidence of the high agricultural capability of Israel: one acre of cultivated land in Israel yields up to 30 times more than an acre in a regular agricultural country. This is a huge contribution to the problem of hunger that concerns more than half of mankind, the result of relentless research that aspires for achievements.

_____

(19) masbirim.gov.il

Israel has developed hydrologic methods to grow crops even in the most arid regions. Israel shares this know-how with many countries and nations, including the tribe "hoopy" of Native Indians in Arizona.

Israel is one of the leading countries in the world in the production of seeds and the cultivation of species of fruits and vegetables.

- In the mid-90s, Israeli research institutes led by Prof. Nahum Keidar and Prof. Haim Rabinovitch, developed the cultivar of cherry tomatoes, that has won an international success and is sold all over the world. All the cultivars of tomatoes developed by Prof. Keidar are grown today in dozens of countries around the world, from European countries to Mexico and from South Africa to Morocco and Iran. The seeds of all the cultivars are manufactured only in Israel.

- The "Galia" melons species were developed in Israel in the Volcani Center and have become the leading in Europe.
- The Israeli spices market constitutes 60%-70% of the spices market in Europe.
- With the development of crossbreeding and of genetic engineering, various species of plants have been ameliorated and cultivated in Israel, with a focus on generating fruits and vegetables that are more weatherproof, with a longer shelf life, tastier and seedless (such as seedless watermelons).
- The "Light" citrus species, that are considered the dream of every farmer because of their resistance to diseases, and the fact that they peel easily and have almost no seeds, were developed in Israel in the Volcani Center and are sold all over Europe. The rights to the species have been sold and it is grown in Europe.
- Israel is marketing special species of daffodils and buttercups to Europe.

- Israel has developed species of grapevines for consumption that yield large crops.
- Israel has developed special techniques and species of fruits that grow out of season and are sold in the world, such as: strawberries, persimmons and blackberries.

Israel's many capabilities in the field of agriculture led to that many countries use the novel Israeli technologies.

Israel has contributed enormously to the high-tech industry, to software and to world technology:

Israel occupies a distinguished place in world high-tech and stands alongside the United States with more than 3,000 start-up companies and start-up projects (projects to locate new high-tech products with commercial potentials). In 2008, the year of the global economic collapse, the venture capital investments per capita in Israel were 2.5 times more than in the United States, 30 times more than Europe, 80 time more than Japan and 350 more than India. The number of start-up companies per capita in Israel is the highest in the world: 3,850 – i.e. one company per 1,844 residents. Each year more start-up companies are set up in Israel than in any country in Europe.

The huge "Intel" development centers deserve credit for developments that are breakthroughs in the international Intel, led by the laptop technology Intel® Centrino® that is sold today all over the world. The processors that have been developed in Israel are integrated in almost every computer on earth.

The first anti-virus was developed at the Hebrew University in Jerusalem, in 1988, by three computer experts.

The Firewall technology, developed by the Israeli company "Check Point"a, founded by Gil Shwed, was designed for monitoring data and for blocking computerized communications. The Firewall technology together with the anti-virus, constitute the most important elements in securing computer data.

In 1989 Dov Moran founded the "M System", the company that developed the mobile storage that earned the name "diskonkey" – a tiny data storage device for the computer. This device has different names in different places in the world, the most common one is a Memory Stick.

In 1995, the "VocalTec" company laid the foundations for the VoIP era, phone calls over the internet, and the "Mirabilis" company introduced the first instant messaging software, the ICQ. Further on, the voice mail technology was developed here as well.

Both "Microsoft" and "Crisco" set up in Israel their only research and development centers outside of the USA.

The Microsoft branch in Israel was founded in 1989 and was one of the first   Microsoft branches outside the United States. The operating systems Windows NT and XP were developed by Microsoft-Israel, in addition to a long list of global developments registered in the names of Israeli developers.

PHP – dynamic web development language – developed by Zeev Suraski and Andi Gutmans from the Technion - Israel Institute of Technology.

Developments of international significance were made in Israel also in the field of medicine:

* The Teva Pharmaceuticals in Israel has developed the Copaxone drug for the treatment of multiple sclerosis.

- A kit for diagnosing the "SARS" virus within an hour was developed in Israel. [20]
- The "Medinol" company has developed flexible and durable supporters of the arteries for the treatment of heart diseases (stent).
- The "Given Imaging" company has developed a pill that contains a video camera to photograph the intestines.
- A special syringe for taking blood from premature babies was developed in Israel. The uniqueness of the syringe is that it enables to restore the red blood cells to prevent anemia in premature babies.

(20) Well, it`s no big deal. The despicable Zionists were those who developed the virus in order   to "make money" by selling the vaccines.

- Dr. Gal Yadid, Dr. Rachel Mayan and Prof. Abraham Weizmann from the Bar-Ilan University in Israel, have developed a natural drugs detoxification. The detoxification is performed by inserting a natural steroid to the brain that develops immunity to the drug in the patients.
- The "InSightec" company has developed an ultra-sound system guided by MRI to remove tumors in a non-invasive way.
- The "Vascular" company has developed a "smart" infusion needle that has   a sensor which sounds an immediate vocal indication that the penetration to the vein is correct.
- The "Rimon Medical Technologies" company has developed a tiny sensor that monitors and reports on cardiac functioning by wireless technology.
- The "Notal Vision" company has developed a self-check household device for people

who suffer from AMD [21], to detect any deterioration.

Of course, this is just a taste on the tip of the tongue of the enormous potential that exists in the State of Israel.

The amount of Israeli biotechnological companies is enormous. In the local capital market the stock exchange has allocated a special index that concentrates the leading BioMed companies, and beyond that Israeli companies are traded in the USA as well. Think about the enormous know-how that exists in these companies for developing medicaments, for advanced research in stem cell, for procedures and instruments taken directly out of the future in order to find solutions for diseases or for incurable processes, such as cancer.

The list is endless and encompasses all levels of life. The purpose of the brief list is to show the enormous contribution to humanity of such a small country so lacking in natural resources for the welfare of humanity. If you wish to boycott Israel, stop using any means of technology you own. If you preach to boycott Israel through your cell phones or through your computers, you yourselves are violating the boycott. Stop taking some of your medications, even if you are sick or suffer from some complex disease. It is very likely that some of the recent developments

---

[21] Eye disease that causes a significant decrease in vision and even blindness.

in biotechnology and in medicine were invented in Israel. Throw away your USB flash disk because it was invented by a Zionist. Erase the firewall in your computer that was developed in a Zionist entity, stop eating a big variety of fruits and vegetables since it is likely that some of them were developed in Israel. Instead, use products and substitutes that were developed in Arab countries.

Boycotting the State of Israel is a sweeping denial of its enormous contribution to the welfare of the world. This is spitting into a well from which you drink. The attempts to ignore the scientific research of the State of Israel, the ignorance that leads to boycotting the country that is responsible for so many developments used by everybody without their knowledge, is similar to the burning of Jewish books during the Nazi Germany.

Then, like today, attempts were made to wipe out the rich culture of the Jewish people, and to fill the resulting vacuum with something else. The vacuum that was created in Europe is filling now. The Jews in Sweden who do not feel safe, are now replaced by a population that is probably more suitable in its character to the current Swedish population and that corresponds to the multicultural policy.

I may be about to say something that is not politically correct, but the use of political correctness is turning Sweden by leaps and bounds into a Muslim theocracy. [22] The unwillingness to look at the threat in a direct way is what causes the Swedish culture to dissolve and disappear. The culture (the politically correct) will soon be replaced by a completely different culture that will seek to establish, in the name of multiculturalism, a Republic of a different kind.

So whether you boycott Israel because it is a "conqueror", it imposes "apartheid", it is "aggressive" or a "baby killer", the truth is that you are being fooled! Your innocence is taken advantage of, the fact that you are free citizens and as such exposed to endless information a large part of which is biased and plain propaganda and that is used in order to attempt to overthrow a democracy and establish in its place a shady regime, like the one that was established in the Gaza Strip following Israel`s complete withdrawal from there.

(22) Please read the article through the link: http://www.brusselsjournal.com/node/4097

Remember that currently there are no occupied territories: Israel has withdrawn completely from the Gaza Strip, a large part of the Judea and Samaria is under the control of the Palestinian Authority, and the Golan Heights was conquered from Syria, but it is probable that when the Syrians will want peace, the State of Israel will be glad to give them the Golan Heights. As long as there is a state of war between Israel and Syria, Israel will hold this strategic asset that dominates its entire northern part.

The occupied territories that the Arabs are talking about (and are misleading you) are in fact the territories of the State of Israel: Tel-Aviv, Haifa, Beersheba, Eilat – they want everything! And through a tremendous propaganda network funded by oil money they manage to brainwash innocent citizens!

 — caption continued below:

(23)

---

(23) The picture was taken from the Arabic Wikipedia under the entry: "The map of Palestine". In this entry the role of Israel in the Middle East is also explained: "The Zionists are the reason for instability, war and destruction in the middle east. The only solution to ensure stability in the Middle East is to bring an end to the ruling of the thieves and the terrorists and the return Palestine to the Palestinians." Tell that to the thousands of Muslims slaughtered undisturbed in Syria, Yemen, Lebanon, Egypt, Libya, Tunisia etc.

http://ar.wikipedia.org/wiki/%D8%AE%D8%A7%D8%B1%D8%B7%D8%A9_%D9%81%D9%84%D8%B3%D8%B7%D9%8A%D9%86

If you boycott Israel because it committed a "massacre" in the Gaza Strip, remember that during operation "Cast Lead" 1,400 Palestinians were killed, most of them armed and terrorists who do not recognize the State of Israel and are occupied with a global Jihad against anyone who is not Muslim. Remember that the "Hamas" terror organization is a branch of the "Muslim Brothers", an organization that aims to cleanse the area from the heretics and to implement the laws of Islam in the region. The organization that controls the Gaza Strip through aids from Iran and Syria has been bombing the State of Israel for 9 years using missiles and rockets. Until operation "Cast Lead" it has launched over 9,000 missiles.

MAKES NO SENSE!

And if you ask about the condition of the children in the Gaza Strip, I feel very sorry for them, but unfortunately we cannot do anything. As Golda Meir [24] said in the past: "We will be able to forgive the Arabs for killing our children, but we will   not be able to forgive them for forcing us to kill their children. Peace with the Arabs will prevail when they will love their children more than they hate us."

The children of the Gaza Strip are captives in the hands of the terror organizations that use them as human shields as part of their tactics, they brain wash them and prepare them from infancy for the confrontation with the "brutal Zionist conqueror". You are welcome to confront your opinions regarding the use of human shields. You are welcome to watch movies under the titles: "Hamas using children as human shield" (I only hope that by then they will not be censored because the movies offend the feelings of the Palestinians).

---

(24) Golda Meir (Meyerson) (May 3rd 1898 – December 8th 1978) was the fourth Prime Minister of Israel and the only woman who has served in this office.

It seems   From the Hamas day-camp 2010   that the

inspiration for that is provided by children–soldiers that have been trained in Africa through brainwashing and lies.

The terror organization uses the weakness of democracy in order to penetrate it and damage it. Some of the terrorists have no external characteristics and merge in the civilian population, so that it is extremely difficult to locate them.

And what about boycotting because of harming innocent civilians? The answer to that is that this is a defensive war, forced on the country that has reached out its hand repeatedly for peace and time and again the hand was cut off. [25]

The Hamas and the terror organizations arrange the shooting from areas crowded with children and with innocent civilians, knowing that if the IDF responds, innocent people will be hit, and that will arouse public opinion against Israel.

The photo shows a direct hit of a rocket launched from the Gaza Strip that destroyed completely a classroom in a Jewish school in Be'Er Sheva during operation Cast Lead. If there were pupils in school that day, it is likely that there would have been many dead and injured among them. During the Cast Lead operation schools were closed down in the towns and in the cities that suffered rocket attacks , and thus many disasters were avoided. Photographed on 31.12.08 during Cast Lead.

Credit: paffairs_sanfrancisco

The terror organizations have murdered so far thousands of Israelis, babies and mothers, and the world keeps silent. During the "Cast Lead" operation, the terror organizations launched missiles toward Israeli schools and kindergartens. On the other hand, the terror organizations made sure to hide themselves in schools and in crowded areas, and the IDF has canceled many operations realizing that the terrorists mix in the civilian population.

Remember another thing: the number of Muslim in the world is about 1,600,000,000. We have nothings against them. On the contrary, we reach out our hand for peace, but as long as many of them learn the ways of the Jihad, the lies in school regarding the "The protocols of the Elders of Zion", the endless brain washing of colonialism on Arab lands and not the basic simple fact that Israel constitutes a bit over 0.1% of the Middle East, there will be no peace. As long as governments continue to nurture ignorance, hate and hopelessness as a way of life, the picture will not change for the better. (And thanks to Europe for acting to approve the labeling of products manufactured beyond the Green Line).

There is no country in the world that has made so many gestures to entities that seek to destroy it. It is like reaching out a hand for peace to al-Qaeda. The platform of Hamas and the platform of the Palestinian Authority do not recognize Israel's right to exist.

You tell me: is it possible to make peace with them? I wish!

There is no doubt that reality exceeds imagination. In May 2011 it was published that in a Scottish district named West Dunbartonshire a decision was made to boycott Israeli products out of solidarity with the Palestinians [26]. During the period in question coup attempts have been made in several countries throughout the Middle East. In Libya Gaddafi was massacring the civilian population, in Syria the President unleashed his army against innocent civilians. Is it necessary to mention what was happening in Yemen?

_____

_____

(26)   http://cifwatch.com/2011/06/20/uk-jews-fight-dunbartonshire-boycott-discovered-nothing-is-produced-there/   ,"UK   Jews   fight   Dunbartonshire boycott, discovered nothing is produced there".

But those residents in the district are concerned, of course, about their Palestinian brothers, whose rights are blatantly trampled by the Zionists. The leader of the boycott, James Bolan, has expressed his support in Hamas and argued that the members of the organization are "freedom fighters". Article 7 in the Covenant of those freedom fighters speaks about the desire to fulfill Allah's pledge [27]: "Judgment Day will not arrive until the Muslims fight the Jews. When a Jew hides behind rocks and trees, the rocks and trees will call to the Muslim – Hey Muslim, slave of Allah, a Jew is hiding behind us, come and kill him" – a Jew, not a Zionist, no matter what his age or gender.

It should be mentioned here that this is a religious war, Muslims against Jews (and against Christians as well). The use of the word Zionists is just an excuse to join the anti-Semitics among the Christian heretics, since article 22 in the Covenant speaks both about the capitalists and about the communists: "The imperialist forces in the capitalist West (it seems that it refers also to that godforsaken   district in Scotland) and in the communist East support the enemy with all their might and resources. These forces tend to take turns in that job. The day Islam emerges, the heretic forces will unite (meaning everybody) in a war against it, because the heretics are of one nation."

This is yet the sane part of the story. Later on, Jewish activists in Britain were outraged about it and decided to boycott any product manufactured in the district, but their mission failed miserably.

Why? Because the region does not produce anything, or it manufactures plenty of nothing.

---

(27) http://avalon.law.yale.edu/20th_century/hamas.asp

The residents of the district are concerned about the residents of the besieged Gaza Strip, who are forbidden to receive medications, food, blankets and basic humanitarian supplies.

While life expectancy of men in the besieged, bruised, stricken with disease and hunger Gaza Strip, is 71 years, in the thriving district in Scotland life expectancy is only 70 years.

Bizarre but true, and about that it was said:

MAKES NO SENSE!

I could not believe that an entire district does not produce anything. I initiated a search of my own and you are welcome to see what I found in the following picture:

And if some of you are still not convinced and think that the entire chapter is but a Zionist propaganda, I have assembled for you in a table a basic list of companies that must be boycotted. I assembled the companies from websites that promote boycotts of the State of Israel:

http://www.missionislam.com/images/frontpage/boycott.htm

http://www.inminds.co.uk/boycott-israel.html

http://he.scribd.com/doc/6978919/Boycott-Israel-Company-List

https://musliminsuffer.wordpress.com/2009/01/14/alphabetized-boycott-list-of-israeli-corporationsaffiliates-and-banking-institution/

Hereinafter is the list, enjoy:

			GIORGIO ARMANI
MARKS & SPENCER	LANCÔME PARIS		DONNAKARAN NEW YORK

	ALLIBERT		
VICTORIAS SECRET VICTORIA'S SECRET	RIVER ISLAND	TOMMY HILFIGER	VICHY LABORATOIRES

Remember this is a very partial list. If you wish to implement the boycott fully, I suggest that you study the subject in depth, since it is likely that in most computers, cellular, technological, medical, transportation and agricultural products a Zionist product is hiding! You have been warned!

To deepen the understsanding of the Middle East I welcome you to read the series of books I wrote on this matter.

You can find them under my name Kobi Shashoua On Amazon or on the website:
www.kobisha.com

Please feel free to contact me via email:
kobimnsil@gmail.com
Tel: 972-54-8030648

Sincerel,

Kobi Shashoua

In this book I shall reveal to you the hypocrisy that is inherent in the whole issue of apartheid and the witch-hunt that is going on around the State of Israel, out of the intent to harm it in any possible way even at the expense of the Palestinians. After all, the core of the conflict is not about "occupied territories" since the area of the State of Israel is 0.15% of the area of the Middle East; this is a religious war, the same religious war that is taking place on the poor and innocent European soil, that is doing everything in its power to weaken the State of Israel by boycotts, denunciations, and donations to Muslim "charities" that use this money to acquire weapons and enthusiastic soldiers.

And if, however, I did not manage to convince you about the lie machine and the propaganda that are raging against the tiny Jewish state, the only democracy in the Middle East, the ancient homeland of the Jewish people for over 3,000 years, 1,600 before Mohammad came to the world, then you are welcome to boycott Israel, and in order to do this in an optimal way I attach a guide that will teach you how to boycott the State of Israel. Read it to the end and then boycott as much as you want please!

Kobi Shashoua is an author and lecturer. He wrote the most comprehensive book to date regarding the Israeli-Palestinian conflict, "Israel: the truth, the whole truth and nothing but the truth." This book leads the reader chapter after chapter through the complex reality of the conflict and dissects the reasons for the crisis, it reveals to the reader the true faces of the parties involved, presents the tactics, the strategies and the real goals, those that lie underneath the surface. The author also wrote the book series "Facts you must know about the Middle East." The book you are holding now is from that series.

The author, who lives in Israel, the most dangerous neighborhood in the world in the heart of the Middle East, shares with us the facts together with the unique insights and understanding of the region where he lives. We welcome you to participate in this journey from a safe distance.